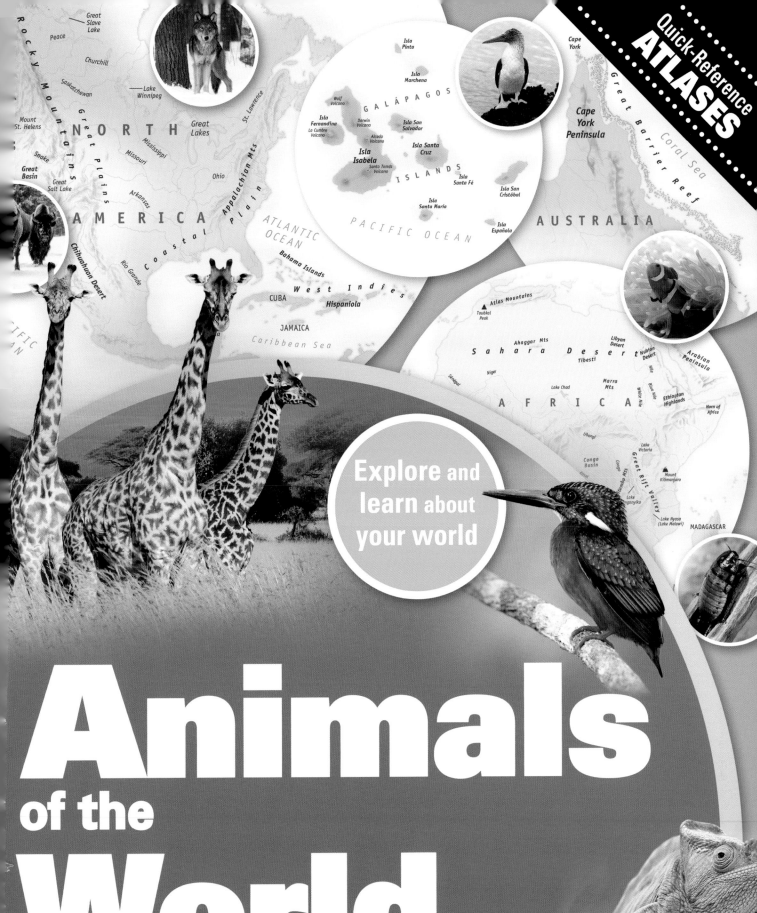

Explore and learn about your world

Animals
of the
World

Author:
Toby Reynolds

Editorial director:
Kathy Middleton

Editor:
Wendy Scavuzzo

Proofreader:
Rodelinde Albrecht

Cover and interior design:
Green Android Ltd

Print and production coordinator:
Katherine Berti

Library and Archives Canada Cataloguing in Publication

Reynolds, Toby, author
    Animals of the world / Toby Reynolds.

(Quick-reference atlases)
Includes index.
Issued in print and electronic formats.
ISBN 978-0-7787-5038-3 (hardcover).--
ISBN 978-0-7787-5048-2 (softcover).--
ISBN 978-1-4271-2147-9 (HTML)

    1. Zoogeography--Juvenile literature. 2. Animals--Juvenile literature. 3. Animal ecology--Juvenile literature. 4. Habitat (Ecology)--Juvenile literature. I. Title.

QL101.R49 2018   j591.9   C2018-902483-6
                                  C2018-902484-4

Library of Congress Cataloging-in-Publication Data

Names: Reynolds, Toby, author.
Title: Animals of the world / Toby Reynolds.
Description: New York, New York : Crabtree Publishing Company, 2019. | Series: Quick-reference atlases | Includes index.
Identifiers: LCCN 2018021427 (print) | LCCN 2018025898 (ebook) | ISBN 9781427121479 (Electronic) | ISBN 9780778750383 (hardcover) | ISBN 9780778750482 (pbk.)
Subjects: LCSH: Animals--Atlases--Juvenile literature. | Zoogeography--Juvenile literature. | Habitat (Ecology)--Juvenile literature. | Children's atlases.
Classification: LCC QL46 (ebook) | LCC QL46 .R49 2019 (print) | DDC 590.9--dc23
LC record available at https://lccn.loc.gov/2018021427

Crabtree Publishing Company

www.crabtreebooks.com   1-800-387-7650
Published in 2019 by Crabtree Publishing Company

First published in Great Britain in 2013 by Green Android Ltd
Copyright © Green Android Ltd 2013

Published in Canada
Crabtree Publishing
616 Welland Ave.
St. Catharines, Ontario
L2M 5V6

Published in the United States
Crabtree Publishing
PMB 59051
350 Fifth Avenue, 59th Floor
New York, New York 10118

Created and produced by:
Green Android Ltd
49 Beaumont Court
Upper Clapton Road
London E5 8BG
United Kingdom
www.greenandroid.co.uk

Please note that every effort has been made to check the accuracy of the information contained in this book, and to credit the copyright holders correctly. Green Android Ltd apologise for any unintentional errors or omissions, and would be happy to include revisions to content and/or acknowledgements in subsequent editions of this book.

Printed in the U.S.A./082018/CG20180601

About this atlas

This *Animal Atlas* has been arranged by continents and regions. Each page contains maps, photographs, information, and facts. Learn about a wide variety of animals that are found in each region, and discover how some animals have **adapted** to survive in their **habitat**. This book takes you from emperor penguins in the freezing Antarctic to jaguars in the steamy rain forests of the Amazon.

Key to the maps

Use the symbols below to identify the main physical features of a continent, country, or region on the maps.

 River

 Mountain

 Lake

 Volcano

 Mountain range

Contents

Animal groups

The animal kingdom can be divided into six basic animal groups. Each animal group is made up of animals that are alike in important ways. Every kind of animal belongs to one of the groups. Sometimes the animals in each group can look very different from each other. An understanding of the main groups of animals will provide you with a good foundation for further learning about the exciting animals on our planet.

The Arctic tern is famous for undertaking the longest **migration** of any bird. It travels from the Arctic to Antarctica each year.

Amphibians

There are more than 7,800 species of amphibians on Earth. Frogs and toads make up the largest order of amphibians. Their **larvae** mature in water and breathe through gills, while the adults breathe air.

Characteristics of amphibians
- Have a backbone or spine
- Are **cold-blooded**
- Have gills for part of their lives
- Live on land and in water

European green toad

Mammals

There are more than 5,400 species of mammals on Earth. They are among the most intelligent of all living creatures. Mammals can be found in land and water habitats.

Characteristics of mammals
- Have a backbone or spine
- Are **warm-blooded**
- Have lungs and breathe air
- Produce milk to feed **offspring**
- Have hair or fur

Black bear

Perentie

Reptiles

There are more than 10,000 species of reptiles on Earth. Most live on land, but some also spend a great deal of time in water. Reptiles are found in most habitats except for polar ice and **tundra**.

Characteristics of reptiles
- Have a backbone or spine
- Are cold-blooded
- Have skin that is covered by scales

Snowy owl

Birds

There are about 18,000 bird species on Earth. Some sources say that as many as 5,000 bird species migrate, or move from one habitat to another. Bird migration is usually done at regular times, according to the seasons.

Characteristics of birds
- Have a backbone or a spine
- Have lungs and breathe air
- Have feathers and a bill
- Lay eggs

Great white shark

Invertebrates

There are more than 1.3 million species of invertebrates living in habitats everywhere on Earth. Invertebrates include insects, spiders, worms, coral, **crustaceans**, and mollusks.

Characteristics of invertebrates
- Do not have a backbone or a spine
- Are cold-blooded

Fish

There are more than 33,000 known species of fish on Earth, although scientists believe there are many more undiscovered fish in our oceans. Fish can be found in all **aquatic** habitats.

Characteristics of fish
- Live in water
- Have a backbone
- Breathe using gills

Monarch butterfly

Animal habitats

A habitat is the environment that provides shelter and food to a community of plants and animals. Although animal life is richest in warm and moist conditions such as the **tropics**, some animals have adapted to life in harsh climates such as hot deserts, high mountains, deep oceans, or frozen ice caps. A habitat may contain and support just a few species or many thousands of species that all live in the same shared space.

Polar bears are adapted to suit a cold environment. They have a layer of fat under their skin, and thick fur to help them stay warm.

Polar and tundra

Polar and tundra are the coldest of all habitats. Compared to other habitats, these icy environments are home to a very small number of animals.

Coniferous forests

Coniferous forests are made up of evergreen trees. These **hardy** trees can survive extreme weather conditions.

Deciduous forests

These areas contain broad-leaved trees such as oak, beech, and elm. They occur in places with high rainfall, warm summers, and cooler winters.

Grasslands

Grasslands are areas with tall grasses and not many trees. Grasslands can support a wide variety of animal life.

Scrublands

Scrublands are dry and hot during the summer. Cool, moist winters prevent them from becoming deserts. They are covered with low bushes and **shrubs**.

Deserts

Deserts are dry places that receive little rain. They are tough places to survive. Desert animals often have special adaptations to help them live here.

Rain forests

These **unique** habitats are hot, humid, and densely packed with vegetation. Rain forests contain a larger range of plant and animal life than any other habitat.

Marshland and swamp

These wetlands are found all over the world. They are home to numerous species of fish, birds, and reptiles.

Mountains

Mountain habitats vary dramatically. At the top, the temperatures are colder, there is less oxygen, and sunlight is harsher. Most mountain animal species live in the lower altitudes.

Coral reefs

Reefs are found mostly in the tropics. They grow in light-filled shallow waters. Reefs provide homes for many aquatic animals.

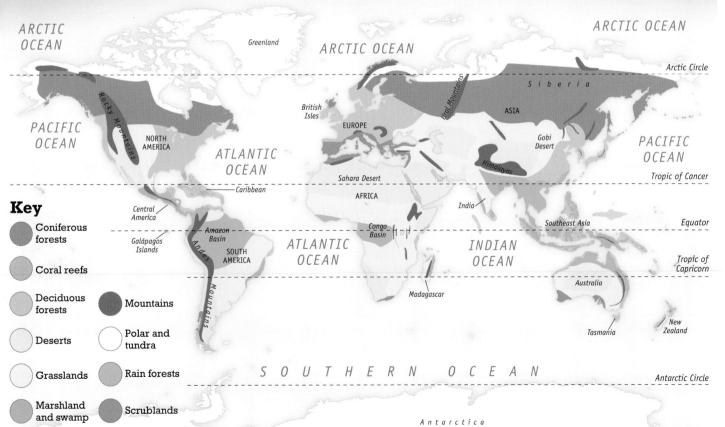

Key

- Coniferous forests
- Coral reefs
- Deciduous forests
- Deserts
- Grasslands
- Marshland and swamp
- Mountains
- Polar and tundra
- Rain forests
- Scrublands

ARCTIC OCEAN
Greenland
ARCTIC OCEAN
ARCTIC OCEAN
Arctic Circle
Siberia
British Isles
EUROPE
ASIA
PACIFIC OCEAN
Rocky Mountains
NORTH AMERICA
ATLANTIC OCEAN
Ural Mountains
Gobi Desert
PACIFIC OCEAN
Sahara Desert
AFRICA
Himalayas
Tropic of Cancer
Caribbean
Central America
India
Galápagos Islands
Amazon Basin
Andes Mountains
SOUTH AMERICA
ATLANTIC OCEAN
Congo Basin
Southeast Asia
Equator
INDIAN OCEAN
Tropic of Capricorn
Madagascar
Australia
Tasmania
New Zealand
SOUTHERN OCEAN
Antarctic Circle
Antarctica

North America

North America is the third-largest continent in the world. It contains many different ecosystems. There are **evergreen** woods, deserts, swamps, lakes, rivers, snowcapped peaks, and beautiful sandy beaches. The variety of environments and climates is reflected in its **diversity** of animals. The bald eagle, Utah prairie dog, American bison, and Gila monster are examples of animals that are unique to North America.

Pack runners

5

Coyotes are relatives of wolves and dogs. They live in packs and hunt small mammals such as voles, prairie dogs, ground squirrels, and mice. To easily tell a coyote from a wolf or dog, watch its tail. A coyote runs with its tail down.

Coyote

White head

1

Bald eagle

Bald eagles have a white head and tail and a brown body. Their sharp eyesight allows them to spot prey far away. When flying, their wings rarely flap. Instead, they soar, holding their wings in a flat and still position.

ARCTIC OCEAN

Yukon

Mount McKinley ▲

Great Bear Lake

Mackenzie

Great Slave Lake

2

PACIFIC OCEAN

Coast Mountains

R o c k y   M o u n t a i n s

Peace

1

Saskatchewan

Chur

Silent hunter

2

The Canada lynx is slightly bigger than a **domestic** cat and has black tufts on its ears. It makes dens in fallen forest trees and sneaks up and catches snowshoe hares, its favorite food.

Canada lynx

3

Utah prairie dog

Barking burrower

Prairie dogs are burrowing rodents that eat vegetation and some insects. They are sociable creatures that live in colonies. Lookouts bark a warning if a predator comes near the colony.

A herd of American bison in Yellowstone National Park.

Mount St. Helens ▲

Cascade Range

Great Basin

Snake

Great Salt Lake

Colorado

4

G r e a t

N

A   M

Baja California

Sierra Madre Occiden

Chihuahuan Dese

Huge herds

4

Herds of bison roam some of the national parks and **reserves** in North America. Their fur coat offers protection in extreme weather. Their shaggy winter coat is so well insulated that snow on their backs does not melt.

Fact

North America is the only continent that has every kind of climate from the dry bitter cold of the Arctic to the steamy heat of the tropics.

American bison

6 Water crawler

The snapping turtle has hardly changed from its ancestor of 215 million years ago. Although it spends most of its life in ponds and rivers, this turtle crawls on the riverbed rather than swiming over it.

Common snapping turtle

7 Changes habitat

The red-spotted newt is an unusual **amphibian** because it leaves the water during its first stage of development. After 2–3 years living on land, it will return as an adult to the water to breed. It remains there for the rest of its life.

Red-spotted newt

8 Howling packs

The largest of the wild dogs, wolves live and hunt in packs of 7–8 animals. Each wolf has a unique howl. They can be heard at dawn, at dusk, and on bright nights when they are most active.

Gray wolves

Deciduous forests of North America

GREENLAND

Hudson Bay

Canadian Shield

Lake Winnipeg

NORTH Great Lakes

St. Lawrence

Mississippi

Missouri

Ohio

Arkansas

Appalachian Mts

Coastal Plain

ATLANTIC OCEAN

RICA

Grande

Gulf of Mexico

Bahama Islands

West Indies

CUBA

Hispaniola

BARBADOS

JAMAICA

Yucatan Peninsula

Caribbean Sea

Lake Nicaragua

Central America

A sandy beach on the island of Barbados, in the Caribbean

9 Insect eater

An armadillo uses its strong legs and front claws to burrow and to dig for food. It has a diet of insects and can eat 40,000 ants in one sitting! Unlike some other armadillos, the nine-banded species cannot roll into a ball.

Nine-banded armadillo

10 Threatening mouth

The cottonmouth is a venomous snake that lives in or around water. It displays its white-skinned mouth when threatened, and has a broad triangular head, **elliptical** pupils, and pits between each eye and nostril.

Cottonmouth

Rocky Mountains

The mountains that stretch down the western side of North America are known as The Rockies. There are snow-covered peaks, alpine meadows, and thick forests. The high altitude means the temperature can be very low, so many of the animals found here have thick fur to protect them. There is a vast array of large mammals that live on this mountain range including moose, grizzly bears, black bears, and coyotes.

Hefty hunter **4**

Brown bears lead **solitary** lives, often only gathering to catch salmon. They are very strong swimmers and can reach speeds of 30 miles (48 km) per hour when running down prey such as moose or elk.

Brown bear

Feline predator **1**

The bobcat, named for its short tail, is a patient **nocturnal** hunter that leaps onto its unsuspecting prey of rabbit, hare, and deer. Bobcats are about twice the size of domestic cats.

Bobcat

Fact

The Rocky Mountains actually represent a series of more than 100 separate mountain ranges rather than one uninterrupted chain.

Snow covers the peaks of Mount Elbert in Colorado.

Hovering bluebird

The male mountain bluebird has brilliant blue **plumage**. The female is gray with blue tinges. These thrushes weave grass, bark, and feather nests in trees, and hover just above the ground to find seeds and insects.

Wood frog

Fir and pine trees cover the slopes of the Rockies.

2

Mountain bluebird

Frozen frogs **3**

The wood frog is easily recognized by the black mask that stretches beyond its eyes and by the two ridges that run down its back. During **hibernation**, this frog can freeze and thaw without damaging its body.

Rocky Mountain goats

Hoofed climber **5**

The large Rocky Mountain goat is a skilled climber that can move quickly up steep, rocky terrain. It lives alone in winter and in herds in summer. Males use their horns for defense and to dominate, and often kill, rival males.

Map labels: Alaska, Yukon, Gulf of Alaska, Great Bear Lake, Great Slave Lake, Peace, Lake Athabasca, Athabasca, Churchill, Lake Winnipeg, Saskatchewan, Rocky Mountains, Coast Mountains, Cascade Range, PACIFIC OCEAN, Sierra Nevada, Snake, Great Salt Lake, Colorado, Arkansas, Missouri, Great Plains, NORTH AMERICA

Western deserts

The largest desert in North America is the Great Basin, and to its south is Death Valley, one of the hottest places on Earth. Farther south lie the Mojave and Sonoran deserts. These harsh desert environments can make survival incredibly difficult for most animals. But the animals that live there generally spend the hot days in burrows or under stones, cacti, or other plants, and only come out at night when the air is cooler.

1 Beetle's blood

The desert blister beetle can pop a **blood vessel** in the joint of its leg, causing yellow blood to ooze out. The insect will do this when it thinks it is about to be attacked. The blood smells bad and can cause painful blisters on human skin.

Desert blister beetle

2 Tiny dinosaur

Unlike most desert animals, the collared lizard hides away at night and spends the daytime basking in the sun. It runs on its hind legs and is said to resemble a small dinosaur. It feeds mostly on insects and other lizards.

Collared lizard

3 Poisonous monster

The Gila monster's black and yellow or pink patterning warns other animals to keep away. The Gila and several other lizards produce **venom**. As it chews, the Gila monster's poison flows into its prey's wounds.

Gila monster

4 Double digestion

Jackrabbits are hares, not rabbits. Their oversized ears have great hearing and release heat to help keep jackrabbits cool. To maximize the water from their diet, these hares eat their own droppings!

Black-tailed jackrabbit

Speedy sprinter

Although the roadrunner can fly, it prefers to run along the ground. It can reach speeds of up to 26 mph (42 kph). It uses its long tail as a brake and for steering as it runs. It is only 20 to 24 inches (51 to 61 cm) long, but can kill a rattlesnake.

Fact
The largest desert in North America is the Chihuahuan Desert. It covers an area of about 175,000 square miles (453,248 sq km).

Sand dunes in Death Valley, the hottest area of North America

Great Basin
Great Salt Lake

Death Valley

Mojave Desert

Colorado

Sonoran Desert

PACIFIC OCEAN

Baja California

Gulf of California

Rocky Mts

Rio Grande

Chihuahuan Desert

Sierra Madre Occidental

N O R T H   A M E R I C A

Giant saguaro cacti grow in the Sonoran Desert.

Roadrunner

The Everglades

The Everglades, on the tip of the Florida peninsula, are one of the world's largest expanses of wetlands. This area is made up of marshland, ponds, and islands of trees. The Everglades are rich with animal life. There are more than 430 fish species, 40 amphibian species, 60 reptile species, and 450 bird species. This World Heritage Site has many **endangered** and **threatened** species, and is an important breeding ground for tropical wading birds.

The Everglades

Lake Okeechobee
Caloosahatchee
FLORIDA
Gulf of Mexico
Biscayne Bay
ATLANTIC O...
Florida Bay
Florida Keys
Straits of Florida

Alligators nest in the sawgrass that edges the waterways of the Everglades.

Loggerhead sea turtle

1 Fishing pouch

Though the smallest of all eight species of pelicans, the brown pelican is 3 feet (1 m) in length with a wingspan of more than 6.5 feet (2 m). It skillfully dives into the sea, and scoops up fish and crustaceans in the huge pouch under its beak.

Brown pelican

2 Racing reptiles

Loggerheads are the largest of the hard-shelled turtles. Their strong jaws crack conch and crab shells, but they also eat sea jellies and seaweed. The females travel long distances to lay their eggs on the same sandy beach on which they were hatched.

Fact

The Everglades are the only place where the American alligator and the American crocodile **coexist** in the wild.

Mangrove forests have dense, tangled roots.

3 Prehistoric reptile

This species of black, broad-headed alligator is believed to be more than 150 million years old and once lived with the dinosaurs! There are more than a million of these predators living in Florida alone.

American alligator

4 Seagrass grazers

Manatees migrate to the Everglades to graze on freshwater plants. They are strong, fast swimmers, but prefer cruising over seagrass beds eating. They stay underwater for a long time, but come to the surface to breathe.

West Indian manatee

5 Rosy pink

The roseate spoonbill gets its pink coloring from algae consumed by the crustaceans in its diet. It also eats fish and snails. It sweeps its spoonlike bill, which has a touch receptor, through the water to sift up food.

Roseate spoonbill

Central America and the Caribbean

Mountainous and tropical Central America, which connects North and South America, has the Pacific Ocean to the west and the Caribbean Sea to the east. The Caribbean consists of more than 7,000 islands. There are coral reefs and the water temperature barely changes throughout the year. This **flora** and **fauna** paradise also experiences dramatic volcanic eruptions, earthquakes, and hurricanes.

Hungry hopper **1**

The Cuban tree frog eats almost anything it can catch. Found on trees or on the ground between the shoreline and mountains, it has large sticky toe pads. To reduce water loss, the skin on its head is fused to its skull.

Cuban tree frog

Fighting crab **2**

Caribbean hermit crabs have a large purple claw. These land crabs hide during the day, but scavenge together at night. They will fight violently over empty shells to call home.

Caribbean hermit crab

Snoozing shark **3**

The most common shark in coral reefs of the Caribbean Sea, this large predator can grow to 10 feet (3 m) long. It rests motionless on seabeds or in caves, so is also known as the "sleeping shark."

Caribbean reef shark

Colorful plumage

The resplendent quetzal is one of the world's most beautiful birds. Its striking tail feathers can grow to 3 feet (1 m) in length. It lives in tropical forests and feeds on fruit, insects, and lizards.

Skillful climber **5**

The tamandua anteater **forages** on the ground and in the treetops. Its long tongue probes ant and termite nests for food. The stench produced by its anal gland has earned it the nickname "stinker of the forest."

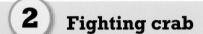
Thick vegetation covers the island of Jamaica.

4
Resplendent quetzal

ATLANTIC OCEAN

Gulf of Mexico

BAHAMAS

1 CUBA

ANTIGUA AND BARBUDA

C E N T R A L   A M E R I C A

GUADELOUPE

▲ *Popocatépetl*

Yucatan Peninsula **2**

JAMAICA

Hispaniola

PUERTO RICO

MARTINIQUE

BARBADOS

Gulf of Honduras

3

C a r i b b e a n   S e a

A N D   T H E   C A R I B B E A N

GRENADA

Gulf of Tehuantepec

4

TRINIDAD

Lake Nicaragua

P A C I F I C   O C E A N

5

Fact
Grenada is a land rich with spices, exotic flowers and rare fruits. It is often referred to as the "Isle of Spice" of the Caribbean.

Gulf of Panama

Many islands were formed by underwater volcanic eruptions.

S O U T H   A M E R I C A

Northern tamandua anteater

South America

This continent is important in the study of animals and their habitats. It was in the Galápagos, for example, that Charles Darwin found evidence for his **theory of evolution**. South America has a wide range of landscapes—deserts, pampas (plains), forests, and mountain ranges. The Amazon, the largest remaining tropical forest, is home to one-tenth of the world's animals, while the Amazon River is the largest basin in the world.

Galápagos Islands

Spectacled bear

Shy and solitary

1 The spectacled bear is an **agile** climber, and will often sit or sleep on platforms high up in the trees of the forest. This shy bear mostly eats vegetation, but will sometimes eat birds, rodents, and insects.

Shaggy coats

2 The llama is a woolly-coated mammal that is native to South America. They are relatives of camels. Llamas are generally intelligent, friendly, and calm animals, but when angered, they are known to hiss, kick, and spit.

Mighty strength

There can be more than five million ants in a leaf-cutter ant colony. The ants can carry leaves that are 50 times their own weight! The leaves fertilize a **fungus**—the colony's only food—which is grown in their underground nests.

Pudu

Pocket-sized deer

4 The pudu is the world's smallest deer, standing up to 16 inches (40 cm) tall. It lives in **temperate** rain forests, and eats plants and fallen fruit. Little is known about this deer. When frightened, a pudu will bark.

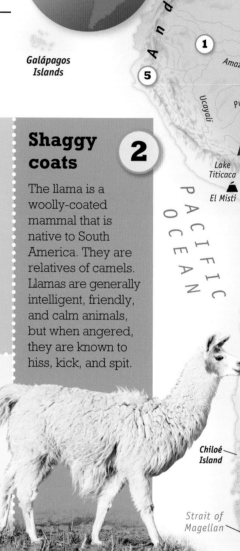

Llama

Leaf-cutter ant

3

Andean condor

Widest wings

5 The Andean condor's wingspan of up to 10.5 feet (3.2 m) is the third-longest in the world. It uses these large wings to soar and glide long distances, looking for dead animals to eat. An Andean condor can live for up to 50 years.

Fact
The Amazon rain forest accounts for more than half of the planet's remaining rain forests. It is one of the most diverse tropical rain forests.

The Amazon River is fed by more than 1,000 **tributaries**.

The Andes Mountains contain peaks more than 19,700 feet (6,000 m) high.

The pampas is mostly dry and barren, and dotted with salt marshes.

6 Leaping feline

Pumas are fierce, swift, and **efficient** hunters that search mountain forests and scrublands for prey. Their bodies are extremely strong. Pumas can leap more than 20 feet (6 m) into a tree. Once in a tree, they will keep climbing!

Puma

7 Mud wallower

The tapir has a flexible nose, like an elephant's trunk. It uses its nose to grasp leaves, twigs, and fruits, and move them into its mouth. A tapir will head to water when chased, and loves **wallowing** in mud.

South American tapir

8 Bold markings

The bumblebee walking toad is a tiny creature with a striking appearance. It has bright yellow spots on the arms, shoulders, and sides. When it feels threatened, it displays the bright red markings on its belly to scare away any predators.

Bumblebee walking toad

9 Magnificent moth

This moth is in the same family as a species that has a 1-foot (30 cm) wingspan! Its wings are colorful and patterned, and the **pupa** is wrapped in a cocoon. The Rothschild atlas moth is found in rain forests and wet grasslands.

Rothschild atlas moth

Appetite for ants 10

The giant anteater uses its huge claws to open mounds, then pokes its 3-foot (1 m)-long sticky tongue inside to lick up the 30,000 ants or termites it needs to eat each day. Though almost blind, it has a great sense of smell.

Giant anteater

Amazon rain forest

The Amazon has existed for 55 million years and is home to thousands of unique species, many yet to be identified. It also contains more than 2.5 million insect species, more than 40,000 plant species, 3,000 edible fruit species, and many life-saving **medicinal plants**. The rain forest is the "lungs of the world," providing one-fifth of the planet's oxygen. Along with the mighty Amazon River, this is a special environment that the world needs to protect.

Rare beauty

1

The jaguar is the largest cat in South America. Its markings **camouflage** it in the forest so it can remain hidden until its prey passes by. Jaguars eat anything from fish and mice to tapirs, and they like to swim!

Jaguar

Fact
More than half of the world's estimated 10 million species of plants, animals, and insects live in this tropical rain forest.

Toco toucan

Massive bill

2

The toco is the largest of all toucans. Though its colorful bill is one-third of the bird's length, it is light because much of it is hollow. The bill is used to reach fruit on twigs that are too small to bear the bird's weight.

Caribbean Sea

—TRINIDAD

Llanos
Orinoco
Guiana Highlands
Negro ①
A m a z o n ④
Amazon ③ Tapajós Amazon
⑤ **B a s i n** ②
Purus Xingu
Madeira
Mouths of the Amazon

SOUTH
AMERICA

Tocantins
São Francisco
Brazilian Highlands

Kapok are the Amazon's tallest trees, growing to nearly 200 feet (60 m).

Andes
Lake Titicaca

PACIFIC OCEAN

ATLANTIC OCEAN

Piranha

The Amazon rain forest receives 59–118 inches (1,500–3,000 mm) of rain each year.

Flesh eaters

3

Piranhas are fierce **predators** with razor-sharp teeth and strong jaws. When big schools of these fish hunt together, they can kill and strip a large animal in a matter of minutes. Their diet also includes snails, fish, plants, seeds, and fruit.

Scarlet macaw

5

Rainbow flier

The scarlet macaw is the second-largest of all South American parrots. It uses its strong, hooked beak to crack Brazil nuts, which are too tough for most birds to crack. It is also able to eat poisonous fruits that would kill other animals.

4

Gripping tails

These acrobatic monkeys move through the **canopy** using their long tails to grip onto tree branches. They are very sociable animals who hug each other as a friendly greeting.

Spider monkey

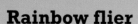

Galápagos Islands

This group of 20 islands and 107 islets is a World Heritage Site, a marine reserve, and a whale **sanctuary**. The area was formed by volcanic activity, which continues to this day. The islands sit more than 560 miles (900 km) west of Ecuador in the middle of five ocean currents, meaning that the water temperature and tides are very unpredictable. These factors have allowed the evolution of some unique species of animals.

Blue-footed booby

1 Clowning around

To find a mate, the male blue-footed booby shows off his colorful feet by performing a strange and comical dance and stamping on the ground. The name "booby" comes from the Spanish word *bobo*, meaning "clown."

2 Ancient reptiles

The Galápagos Islands are home to several species of giant tortoises. These huge creatures are able to survive for long periods of time with very little food or water. They may live to more than 100 years old.

Giant tortoise

Fact
The giant Galápagos tortoises have slightly different physical features depending on which island they come from.

The smaller islands are mainly waterless so few plants survive.

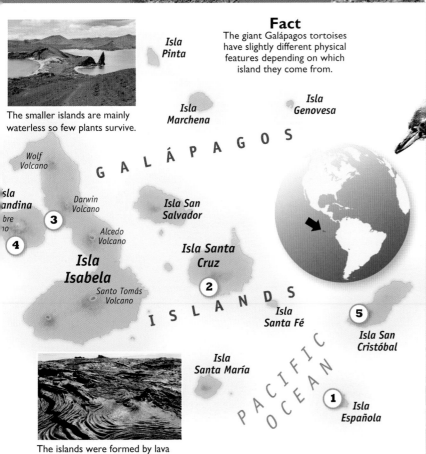

The islands were formed by lava ejected from underwater volcanoes.

Map labels:
Isla Pinta
Isla Marchena
Isla Genovesa
Wolf Volcano
GALÁPAGOS
Darwin Volcano
Isla Fernandina
Alcedo Volcano
Isla San Salvador
Isla Isabela
Santo Tomás Volcano
Isla Santa Cruz
ISLANDS
Isla Santa María
Isla Santa Fé
Isla San Cristóbal
PACIFIC OCEAN
Isla Española

Daytime bathers

These are the only tropical penguins in the world. They are able to survive the hot temperatures by staying in and around cool water currents. They only return to land at night. These same cool waters supply their diet of sardines, mullets, and anchovies.

Galápagos penguin

4 Cactus eaters

Galápagos land iguana

The Galápagos land iguana conserves body heat by sleeping in sandy burrows at night, then basking in the warm sunlight in the mornings. It enjoys a diet of fruit and the pads from prickly-pear cactus. These iguanas can live for 50 to 60 years.

5 Inflatable pouch

The magnificent frigatebird is a very skilled flier. It steals food from other birds or snatches prey from the ocean's surface. To attract a mate, a male inflates its red throat pouch and emits a shrill call.

Magnificent frigatebird

Africa

The huge continent of Africa is home to some amazing animals. Its steamy tropical rain forests shelter many unusual animals, while the world's largest grazing herds roam the continent's vast open **savannahs**. On the island of Madagascar, there are animals that are found nowhere else in the world. In contrast, the Sahara Desert's extreme temperatures and low rainfall is suitable only for the most highly adapted of animals.

Atlas Mounta...
Toubkal Peak
S a h a
Ahag...
Niger
Sénégal
A F
ATLANTIC OCEAN

Feasting flocks

1

Like other vultures, the white-backed vulture is a scavenger that only eats from carcasses of dead animals. Groups of up to 1,000 vultures can surround and feast on the carcass of an elephant, so fights often break out.

White-backed vultures

Rain clouds begin to form at the start of the wet season.

Fact
Africa is the second-largest continent in the world. It covers an area of around 11.7 million square miles (30 million sq km).

2 Rootling around

The warthog uses its wide snout to dig up tasty grass roots. Its diet also includes rodents, insects, eggs, and snakes. Its lumpy face and tusks give it a fierce appearance, but when cornered, the warthog prefers flight to fight.

Monitor lizard on the Nile River

3 Working in pairs

This monitor lizard is 6.5 feet (2 m) long. It can stay underwater for an hour. It will team up with another lizard to get food. While one lizard lures a crocodile away, the other raids its nest and steals its eggs.

4 A ripe old age

Large groups of chimpanzees live in rain forests, woodlands, and grasslands. They feed on fruit, leaves, seeds, bark, and insects, and sometimes hunt for meat. In the wild, they can live to 50 years old.

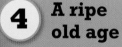
Chimpanzee

Common warthog

Fastest land animal

The cheetah's spotted fur acts as camouflage in the tall dry grass of the plains. It is the fastest land animal, reaching a speed of 75 mph (120 kph) when chasing prey. They are not able to roar, but can purr and meow like domestic cats.

5

Cheetah

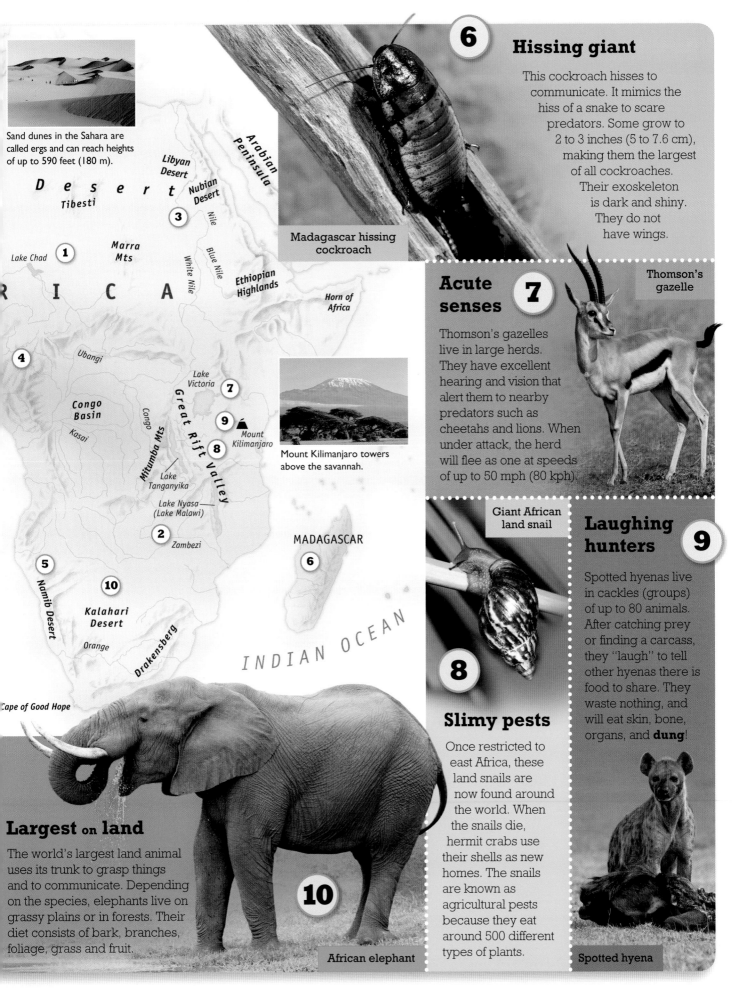

Sand dunes in the Sahara are called ergs and can reach heights of up to 590 feet (180 m).

Tibesti
Libyan Desert
Nubian Desert
Arabian Peninsula
Marra Mts
Lake Chad
Nile
Blue Nile
White Nile
Ethiopian Highlands
Horn of Africa
Ubangi
Congo Basin
Kasai
Congo
Mitumba Mts
Lake Victoria
Great Rift Valley
Mount Kilimanjaro
Lake Tanganyika
Lake Nyasa (Lake Malawi)
Zambezi
MADAGASCAR
Namib Desert
Kalahari Desert
Orange
Drakensberg
Cape of Good Hope
INDIAN OCEAN

Mount Kilimanjaro towers above the savannah.

Madagascar hissing cockroach

6 Hissing giant

This cockroach hisses to communicate. It mimics the hiss of a snake to scare predators. Some grow to 2 to 3 inches (5 to 7.6 cm), making them the largest of all cockroaches. Their exoskeleton is dark and shiny. They do not have wings.

Acute senses 7

Thomson's gazelle

Thomson's gazelles live in large herds. They have excellent hearing and vision that alert them to nearby predators such as cheetahs and lions. When under attack, the herd will flee as one at speeds of up to 50 mph (80 kph).

Giant African land snail

Laughing hunters 9

Spotted hyenas live in cackles (groups) of up to 80 animals. After catching prey or finding a carcass, they "laugh" to tell other hyenas there is food to share. They waste nothing, and will eat skin, bone, organs, and **dung**!

8 Slimy pests

Once restricted to east Africa, these land snails are now found around the world. When the snails die, hermit crabs use their shells as new homes. The snails are known as agricultural pests because they eat around 500 different types of plants.

Largest on land

The world's largest land animal uses its trunk to grasp things and to communicate. Depending on the species, elephants live on grassy plains or in forests. Their diet consists of bark, branches, foliage, grass and fruit.

African elephant

Spotted hyena

Madagascar

Madagascar is the fourth-largest island in the world. It was once attached to Africa's mainland, but the land split off and drifted away millions of years ago. Madagascar has rain forests on the east side of the island. The south of the island is much drier and desertlike. Across the middle of the island is the central plateau, where the weather is much milder and the land is covered in a grassy savannah.

Madagascar tenrec

Sideways hopper

5

The sifaka is a tree-dwelling lemur that spends most of its life in forests. Powerful back legs help the lemur leap from tree to tree. On the ground, they get around by doing a comical sideways hop. They live and forage for food in small troops.

Color changers

1

A chameleon changes the color of its skin for communication and defense, and as a response to temperature, light, and mood. Its eyes move in different directions, and its suction cup tongue can be twice as long as its body.

Parson's chameleon

Spiky forager

4

A tenrec is a small, shy animal. It sleeps in a burrow during the day and forages at night. Its coat consists of spines. It rolls into a ball when threatened and rubs its spines to create a grating sound.

Sifaka

Smelly fighters

2

Lemurs lives in troops of up to 24 members. They are found in the treetops and on the ground eating plants, flowers, and fruit. Males have "stink fights" in which they spread scent on their tails and wave them around!

Ring-tailed lemurs

Grasslands cover much of Madagascar's central plateau.

Betsiboka

5

4

1

Manja

Central Plateau

Mangoky

MOZAMBIQUE CHANEL

INDIAN OCEAN

MADAGASCAR

Sticky feet

3

This gecko is active during the day, unlike other geckos. It eats insects, flower nectar, and fruit. Its long tail aids balance and stores fats. Fine hairs on the toes allow it to walk upside down on almost any surface.

Madagascar day gecko

Madagascar's rain forests are home to a large variety of plants and animals.

Fact

The unique ecology of Madagascar has led some scientists to refer to the country as the "eighth continent" of the world.

Onilahy

2

3

Savannah

The huge African grassy plains are called savannahs. The savannah has two seasons—wet and dry—and it is home to many of the continent's largest mammals. Enormous herds of grazing animals travel around the savannah looking for food. Most animals survive by eating the grasses that grow in the savannah. Each species eats a different part of the grass so they don't compete with each other for food.

African lion

1 Roaring felines

Lions live in large groups. They are meat-eaters who hunt animals ranging from small hares to large buffalo. A male's roar can be heard up to 5 miles (8 km) away. Lions spend most of the day resting in the shade.

Speedy sprinter 2

The ostrich is the tallest and heaviest of all birds. An adult ostrich stands around 9 feet (2.7 m) tall. Its wings are too small for flying, but are used for balancing when it runs at high speeds. The long legs are also useful for kicking predators.

Ostrich

Acacias are one of the most common savannah trees.

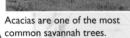

Fact
Some plants store water in their roots, and others extend their roots deep into the ground to get water during the long dry season.

A large herd of wildebeest migrates across the savannah.

Long and tall 3

The giraffe, the tallest animal in the world, uses its height and great eyesight to survey the grasslands for predators. The spindly legs would collapse under its weight were it not for a unique adaptation in its leg bones.

Giraffe

4 Striped horses

Zebras have a pattern of stripes that is unique to each zebra. Beneath the stripes is a white coat and black skin. There are three zebra species in Africa: Burchell's or plains, Grevy's, and the mountain zebra.

Mountain zebras

Enormous grazer 5

The white rhinoceros is known for its wide mouth, huge body, and horns, which can grow to more than 3 feet (1 m) long. It has very poor eyesight but excellent hearing and smelling senses. The white rhino grazes on grasses and likes to wallow in mud.

White rhinoceros

Rain forests and lakes

The tropical rain forests of Africa stretch out from the west coast to the Great Rift Valley. These thick forests are warm and humid, making them a wonderful place for wildlife to thrive. There is plenty of food in the rain forests, with fruits and shrubs growing everywhere. Some animals spend most of their lives high up in the trees, while other animals feed on fallen fruit that litters the forest floor.

1 Tree wrestler

The green mamba only leaves trees to find bird eggs and mammals to eat. It grows to 7 feet (2 m). Its venom is not as toxic as that of the black mamba. To win females for mating, males wrestle each other.

Western green mamba

Chattering flocks

Famous for its ability to mimic other bird calls and humans, the grey parrot is one of the largest parrots in Africa. Large, noisy flocks travel long distances through forests, mangroves, and savannahs to find fruiting trees, nuts, and seeds.

3 Primate families

Gorillas, the largest of all primates, live in troops. They communicate using body postures, facial expressions, and sounds. They eat shoots, stems, fruit, and sometimes worms and insects.

Western lowland gorilla

Floating on vegetation 4

The African jacana uses its large blue bill to forage for insects in the shallow lakes where it lives. Its long thin feet enable it to walk on top of floating vegetation. It lays its eggs in a floating nest.

African jacana

Fact

Rain forests stretch across most of central Africa and are in more than 30 countries. Many of the rain forests outside the Congo Basin have been ruined by commercial exploitation.

Much of Africa's rain forest lies in the basin of the Congo River.

2

African grey parrot

Hippopotamus

Niger

Lake Volta

A F R I C A

Adamawa Mts

Ubangi

ATLANTIC OCEAN

Congo Basin

Congo

Kasai

Lake Tanganyika

Mitumba Mts

Great Rift Valley

Lake Victoria

Mount Kilimanjaro

Muchinga Mts

Zambezi

Lake Nyasa (Lake Malawi)

Keeping cool

5

The hippopotamus stays submerged in rivers to keep cool. It sleeps underwater, only bobbing up to take a breath. A hippo doesn't swim. It walks along the riverbed.

Huge flocks of flamingos live on lakes in the Great Rift Valley.

Sahara Desert

The Sahara is the largest desert on Earth. The scorching sun makes the desert extremely hot during the day, but at night the temperature drops and it becomes bitterly cold. It rarely rains in the desert, so the Sahara is a tough place in which to live. Animals have had to adapt to these harsh conditions. Some hide from the sun in burrows during the day, while others use the sun's warmth to make themselves active.

1 Recycling waste

The dung beetle can move objects 50 times its own weight. It forms a ball of animal dung, then rolls it away and eats it. This beetle recycles most of the world's animal dung back into the soil.

Dung beetle

The Sahara contains several hot, dry mountainous regions where few plants survive.

Saharan horned viper

The Sahara contains rocky **plateaus** called hammadas.

Fact
Strong winds can blow fine dust from the surface of the desert. The dust can be blown as far as Europe and the United States.

2 Smallest fox

Fennec fox

The fennec fox is the smallest of all the foxes. It spends its days in burrows and its nights scavenging for insects and fruit. Its huge ears radiate body heat to keep it cool. The bottoms of its paws are covered in fur to help it cross hot, loose desert sand.

3 Horned reptile

The horned viper is a venomous small snake. The horns are single scales that sit above its eyes. It inhabits rock cliffs, dunes, and dry streambeds. To avoid extreme temperatures, it buries itself in sand with only its head visible.

4 Fatty hump

Arabian camels, also known as dromedaries, have one hump, short hair, and long legs. They last long periods of time without food and water by turning fat stored in their hump into water and energy.

Arabian camel

5 Paralyzing sting

Scorpions have eight legs, large front claws, and a long, segmented tail with a poisonous tip. The poison paralyzes and kills prey. They can survive a year without eating and for a few days without oxygen.

Robust burrowing scorpion

Europe

Europe stretches from the **glaciers** of Iceland in the west to the forests and steppes of Russia in the east, and from Scandinavia in the north to the warm, dry climate of Mediterranean forests, woodlands, and scrub in the south. Europe is bordered on three sides by oceans and seas. There are four main types of habitats within Europe: polar tundra, **deciduous** woodlands, **coniferous** forests, and scrublands.

This **glacier** in Iceland was formed over many years by compressed fallen snow.

Fact
Europe is the second-smallest continent by surface area, but it has the second-largest population at around 750 million people.

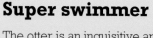

1 Prickly predator

Common hedgehog

A hedgehog has around 5,000 spines on its body. The spines are light and hollow, but very sharp. When scared, it rolls into a ball so predators can't attack without being pricked. Its vision is poor, so it uses hearing and smell when hunting.

2 Super swimmer

The otter is an inquisitive and playful mammal. It lives in and around water. Its slim body, webbed toes, and powerful tail make it an agile swimmer. It lives in holts—hollows underneath riverbanks, logs, and roots.

Eurasian otters

3 Powerful digger

Eurasian badger

These **elusive** animals live in underground homes, called setts, with other badgers. They dig tunnels and chambers for the sett, and dig for their food. Badgers eat several hundred earthworms a night.

The Mediterranean scrubland is covered with thorny shrubs and small trees.

4 Fighting butterfly

Black-veined white butterfly

The black-veined white is a large white butterfly with black veins on its wings. It likes to live in meadows with scrub, or cultivated areas with fruit trees. It will fight with other black-veined whites for space on nectar plants.

Skillful climber

The alpine ibex is well adapted for mountain areas such as the Alps. It is a great climber and can scale almost vertical rock walls. Its sharp-edged hooves have **concave** undersides that act like suction cups.

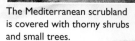

Alpine ibex

North Cape

Lake Region

Lake Onega

Lake Ladoga

Western Dvina

The lakes in the northern European forests provide water for many animals.

European Plain

Central Russian Upland

Vistula

Oder

Dnieper

Dniester

Don

Carpathian Mountains

Danube

Crimea

Black Sea

Balkan

Balkan Mts

Peninsula

Danube

Ionian Sea

Etna

Peloponnese

Sicily

Crete

ASIA

CYPRUS

Mediterranean Sea

6 Fishing from the sky

Osprey

The fish-eating osprey glides over and dives under the water. At the last moment, it pushes its feet forward so the talons grab onto the fish. In the autumn, it leaves Europe and migrates south to warmer weather.

Silent hunting 7

The Eurasian lynx roams forests and is a stealthy hunter that will hide to avoid detection. It can kill animals, such as deer, that are four times its body size. Its large, fur-covered paws help it move through deep snow.

Eurasian lynx

Toxic skin 8

The skin of the fire salamander needs to be kept moist, so it lives near water. It stays hidden during the day. It eats insects, worms, spiders, and slugs, and produces a **toxin** to **deter** predators.

Fire salamander

Bushy tails 9

The red squirrel is built for its life in the trees. Its tail aids balance and its claws grip bark. Found throughout Europe, it has mostly been replaced by gray squirrels in the U.K. and in parts of Italy.

Quiet observer 10

The large grey heron stands patiently in streams and ponds, waiting to stab a passing fish with its sharp beak. Along with fish, it eats frogs, insects, small mammals, and reptiles. In flight, its curved wings make an easy to spot m-shape.

Grey heron

Red squirrel

Asia

Asia is an immense area—one-third of all the land on Earth—and home to 60 percent of the world's population. The extreme north is one of the coldest areas in the world, while the south is hot and wet. Asia has a huge range of habitats, including the high mountains of the Himalayas, Lake Baikal with one-fifth of Earth's fresh water, frozen glaciers, deserts, **steppes**, rivers, oceans, and seas.

Heavy flier

1

The heaviest of all flying animals, the great bustard is 3 feet (1 m) tall and grows whiskers in spring! It does not glide, but flaps its wings slowly. It has no hind claws, so it can't perch in trees. It lives on the ground.

Great bustard

Daily walks

2

Smaller than its African cousin, the Asian elephant has two bumps on its head and smaller ears. A herd will sometimes walk as far as 30 miles (48 km) each day to find water, grasses, fruits, and bark.

Asian elephants

The steppe consists of vast grassland plains where few trees can grow.

EUROPE

Ural Mountains

West Siberian Plain

Black Sea

Caucasus Mts

A S

The Steppes

Aral Sea

Irtysh

Syr Darya

Caspian Sea

Amu Darya

Euphrates

Tigris

Zagros Mountains

Hindu Kush

Indus

6

Himalay

Ku

Arabian Peninsula

Great Indian Desert

Mt Evere

5

Ga

Arabian Sea

3

Deccan Plateau

Scruffy fur

Named for its scruffy coat and shuffling walk, the sloth bear is an active and noisy resident of forests and grasslands. Its claws help it tear open termite and ant nests, and climb trees. It eats fruit when it is in season.

Bactrian camel

Double hump

4

The Bactrian is a two-humped camel with long eyelashes and narrow nostrils, which reduce damage in desert sandstorms. It conserves water by **urinating** and sweating little, and it stores fat in its humps.

Fact

Asia is the largest continent on Earth. It covers almost 9 percent of the globe and just under one-third of the total land mass of the planet.

2

Bay

SRI LANKA

3

Feathery fan

5

The male peafowl, called a peacock, has train feathers that are covered with eyespots and look very pretty. The female, called a peahen, has a shorter train without eyespots. Peafowl eat seeds, fruit, and some **rodents** and lizards.

Sloth bear

Indian peacock

Mangroves grow along the east coast of India and many islands of southeastern Asia.

Bulky grazer

6

Yaks are herd animals found in the mountain regions of central Asia. They can live where other animals would suffer **altitude sickness**. The thick, long coat helps this bulky animal to survive in extremely cold climates.

Yak

The Gobi Desert has mostly rocky terrain with sparse vegetation.

Treetop swinger

8

Built to swing in the treetops, this gibbon can carry things in its hands and feet! Its arms are longer than its legs, so when it walks it puts its hands on its head for balance. It makes loud hooting sounds.

Gibbon

Kingfisher

7

Vivid plumage

This kingfisher is a small, shy bird that retreats to small pools and forests with lots of cover. It has bright blue and orange feathers. It dives almost vertically from overhanging branches into the water to catch fish.

Cunning fisher

9

This heron lives in wetlands and eats fish, crabs, snakes, eggs, and small mammals. It dips its bill into the water and quickly opens and closes it to create a fish-attracting disturbance. This is called bill vibrating.

Black-crowned night heron

10

Night hunting

This pit viper is found only in one small forest and woodland area in Thailand. It is a nocturnal hunter that eats mammals and birds. It hides in the dry season and comes out in the wet season.

Kanburi pit viper

Chukchi Peninsula

Bering Sea

Klyuchevskaya Sopka

Kamchatka Peninsula

Verkhoyansk Range

Central Siberian Plateau

Lena

Sea of Okhotsk

Kurile Islands

Amur

Lake Baikal

1

Mongolian Plateau

ntains

Gobi Desert

Yellow

Sea of Japan

JAPAN

4

North China Plain

East China Sea

Yangtze

Ryukyu Islands

bet

Brahmaputra

9

Taiwan

Salween

Mekong

Hainan

South China Sea

Philippine Islands

gal

10

Indochina Peninsula

PACIFIC OCEAN

New Guinea

Borneo

Sulawesi

Arafura Sea

7

Sumatra

I N D O N E S I A

Java Sea

8

Java

INDIAN OCEAN

AUSTRALIA

Siberia

Siberia, in eastern Russia, is one-tenth of Earth's land surface. It contains Lake Baikal, the oldest and deepest lake in the world, which is home to 570 plant species and 1,340 animal species, including the Baikal seal. Siberia is mostly pine forests. The cold temperature and very little vegetation make it a very difficult place for animals to live in year-round unless they hibernate or have a thick coat.

Lake Baikal is the deepest lake in the world, reaching depths of 5,387 feet (1,642 m).

Fact
Yakutsk in Siberia is said to be the coldest city on Earth. The average January temperature is around -43.5 °F (-40 °C), though it can be hot in summer.

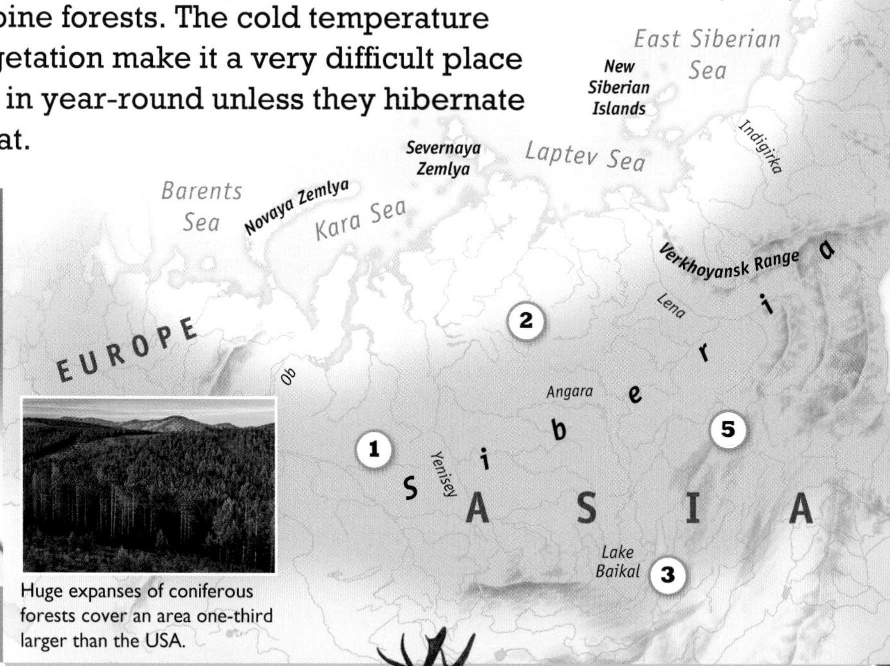

1 Striped rodent

Siberian chipmunk

Huge expanses of coniferous forests cover an area one-third larger than the USA.

This chipmunk has striking fur with five dark and four light bands running down its back toward its fluffy tail. It lives in burrows in many habitats and hibernates in winter. It competes with squirrels and voles for food, and raids nests for eggs.

Reindeer

2 Winter survival

A reindeer has several adaptations for winter survival. Its nose has many blood vessels for blood flow and temperature regulation. Hoof pads shrink so the hard rims cut into the ice for grip and to dig for lichens to eat.

Ural owl

3 Freshwater seal

This seal is unique to Lake Baikal. It can dive to 1,312 feet (400 m) and stay under water for 70 minutes. It winters under the ice, keeping air holes open. It feeds at night when fish swim up from the depths.

Baikal seal

Thick fur coat 4

The male Siberian tiger grows to 11 feet (3.3 m) long! It has extra thick fur and a mane to help it survive the freezing cold winters. Food is scarce so it hunts a lot, stalking wild boar, elk, deer, bears, and small animals.

Siberian tiger

5 Night hunter

The Ural owl has a large round head, small black eyes, and no tufts. It hunts mostly at night for mammals, frogs, and insects, and stores extra food in a hiding place. It **roosts** in tree trunks by day.

Map labels: Barents Sea, Novaya Zemlya, Kara Sea, Severnaya Zemlya, Laptev Sea, New Siberian Islands, East Siberian Sea, Indigirka, Verkhoyansk Range, Sea of Okhotsk, Sakhalin, Lena, Angara, Yenisey, Ob, Sea of Japan, JAPAN, EUROPE, ASIA, Siberia, Lake Baikal

Himalayas

This enormous mountain range contains Mount Everest—the highest point in the world! The Himalayas act as a climate barrier, stopping cold weather moving down to India and central Asia, and blocking **monsoon rains** moving north to the **arid** deserts. The peaks are always snow-capped, while lower elevations can be mild and forested. Most animals hibernate to survive the winters high in the range; the rest migrate to lower areas.

Flying scavenger (1)

With a wingspan of just over 10 feet (3 m), this vulture soars on warm air (thermals) since it is unable to flap for long periods. It feeds on the flesh of dead animals. A party of vultures can strip a yak in two hours.

Himalayan griffon vulture

(2)

Alpine chough

Two-tone coat (3)

Found in mountains and jungles, the Asiatic black bear has a white V on its chest and a furry neck ruff. Its diet varies seasonally, but it mostly feeds on nuts such as acorns and fruits such as berries.

Fact

The Himalayas stretch over 75 percent of Nepal. Of the world's ten highest mountain peaks, nine are contained within the Nepalese Himalayas.

The summit of Mount Everest is 29,030 feet (8,848 m) high.

Spinning acrobat

The alpine chough performs acrobatic tumbles and spins at high altitudes. It nests at record heights for a bird. It will dig the ground with its beak to find insects and larvae. It will also scavenge trash.

Asiatic black bear

ASIA

Himalayas

CHINA

Plateau of Tibet

Indus   Sutlej

Ganges

Great Indian Desert

INDIA

Mt Everest ▲

Brahmaputra

(2) (1) (3) (4) (5)

Trees on the mountains soak up rain and hold the soil together.

Deccan Plateau

Mouths of the Ganges

Bay of Bengal

Impressive horns (4)

The Markhor goat has magnificent twisted horns that can grow to more than 5 feet (1.5 m). It lives on rocky **outcrops** above the tree line. Its coat varies with the changing seasons, but males have a beard and shaggy mane.

Markhor goat

Insulated fur

Highly adapted to its cold snowy home, the snow leopard has large paws, short front, and a woolly underlayer to its long fur. It wraps its long thick tail around itself for extra warmth.

Snow leopard

(5)

East Asia

East Asia includes China, Mongolia, North and South Korea, Japan, and Taiwan. Climates in this region fall into two categories. Some areas have warm-to-hot summers and mild winters; others have hot summers followed by very cold winters. The Gobi Desert is a cold desert with frost and occasional snow. The Korean **peninsula**, Japan, and Mongolia are mostly mountainous areas with some volcanic activity.

1

Bushy tail

Red pandas—related to raccoons and weasels—are agile treetop climbers. When cold, they cover themselves with their bushy tail. They eat bamboo, berries, eggs, and some small mammals.

Red panda

2

Tree amphibian

The Japanese tree frog grows up to 1.8 inches (4.5 cm), lives on the water's edge, and breeds in rice fields. It hunts during the night and seeks out light, even street lights, that attracts its insect prey.

Japanese tree frog

3

Bamboo chewing

The giant panda lives in bamboo forests. It has opposable thumb pads to grasp bamboo, and strong jaws and teeth to crush it. It can climb and swim. Though peaceful, it will fight predators if it needs to.

Giant panda

Snow monkey

4

The snow monkey or Japanese macaque has a hairless red face, and it lives in mountainous areas and forests. Its coat thickens for the bitter cold winters. Troops of macaques often bathe in volcano-heated spring water.

Japanese macaque

Japanese deer

5

This deer lives in woodland, bogs, and salt marshes, but a herd of more than 1,000 have made their home in a town in Japan, unworried by cars or people. They run swiftly, jump, and swim. The male rubs its antlers on trees to mark its territory.

Sika deer

MONGOLIA

Gobi Desert

Woodlands cover about 70 percent of Japan's land area.

Hokkaido

Sea of Japan

Honshu

5

2

Korean Peninsula

Mount Fuji

JAPAN

Qinghai Hu

Yellow

A S I A

North China Plain

Yellow Sea

C H I N A

Yangtze

East China Sea

3

1

PACIFIC OCEAN

Ryukyu Islands

Taiwan

Xi Jiang

South China Sea

Fact

China is the fourth-largest country in the world after Russia, Canada, and the USA. It has an area of 3.6 million square miles (9.3 million sq km).

The Yellow River flows across China. It contains a lot of silt, making it yellow coloured.

India and Southeast Asia

This region has a wide range of ecosystems and habitats that includes forests, wetlands, grasslands, coasts, marshes, and deserts. The climate is tropical, and monsoons rage during the rainy season. The seas and oceans are as important as the landmasses for wildlife and climate. The seas are mostly shallow, warm, and not very salty, but there are some extremely deep ocean trenches.

1 Menacing reptile

The Komodo dragon is the biggest and heaviest lizard, growing to 10 feet (3 m). It eats almost anything—deer, water buffalo, pigs, or any dead animal it finds. It uses its long yellow forked tongue to taste and smell the air.

Komodo dragon

Woodlands in northern India are home to many animals.

Fact
Kanchenjunga is the world's third highest mountain. Its summit is 28,170 feet (8,586 m) high and it sits on the Nepal–India border.

King cobra

2 Poisonous bite

A king cobra grows to 18 feet (5.5 m) long. It is the longest venomous snake. Its venom can bring down an elephant! Before striking, it rises up, opens the hood below its head, growls, and flicks out its tongue.

The lowland rain forest of Borneo supports more than 10,000 species of plants.

3 Treetop swinger

The orangutan is a large gentle red ape. It is one of humankind's closest relatives, and spends most of its life in the trees of rain forests. Its long arms and hook-shaped hands and feet allow it to climb and swing from tree to tree.

Orangutan

5 Jumping monkey

This strange-looking monkey lives in the jungles of Borneo. The male has a large nose, which is used to **amplify** its loud call. It is an agile tree climber and will leap 50 feet (15 m) from overhanging branches into water.

Proboscis monkey

Killer claws

The cassowary can't fly but can run, jump, and swim. It defends itself by kicking and cutting its opponent with daggerlike claws on its feet. It has a brightly colored face, and neck wattles topped with a bony helmet.

4

Cassowary

Map labels: Ganges, Narmada, INDIA, Godavari, Krishna, Kangchenjunga, ASIA, Irrawaddy, Salween, Mekong, Hainan, South China Sea, Philippine Islands, Bay of Bengal, Andaman Sea, SRI LANKA, Malay Peninsula, Borneo, PACIFIC OCEAN, New Guinea, Sumatra, Sulawesi, INDONESIA, Java Sea, Arafura Sea, Java, Semeru, Timor Sea, AUSTRALIA, INDIAN OCEAN

Australia and New Zealand

One-fifth of Australia is desert. From north to south there are rain forests, deserts, cool forests, and snow-covered mountains. Offshore, there are thousands of islands, including those in the Great Barrier Reef. Eighty percent of the flora and fauna is unique, due to the continent's long isolation. Consisting of three main islands and more than 700 offshore islands, New Zealand has fertile coastal plains, rain forests, and mountain ranges.

Spikes and horns

1

The thorny devil is covered with dragon-like spines and horns. It lives in arid areas and changes color to match its environment. Channels all over its body collect dew from sand and funnel it to the lizard's mouth.

Thorny devil

2 Hungry for termites

The numbat is a small **marsupial** that survives on a diet of mostly termites. An adult eats up to 20,000 termites each day. It has strong front claws and a long tongue, which it uses to get termites out of their nests.

Numbat

Uluru in Australia is the world's largest free-standing rock.

Sand burrower

The bilby has a long pointy nose and huge ears. It eats spiders, insects, fruits, and seeds. It digs long burrows for sleeping and nesting. Its pouch opens backward to keep dirt from getting in as it digs.

Noisy squawkers

4

Flocks of pink and grey galahs make a spectacular sight. They are found across the continent, except in some rain forests. They are known for making a racket with their high-pitched screeching.

Galahs

Swimming senses

5

A platypus is about the size of a cat and has webbed feet for swimming. When in water, it closes its eyes and relies on **sensors** in its bill to locate larvae, insects, and worms in ponds and freshwater rivers.

Platypus

3

Bilby

Arafu

Timor Sea

Arnhem Land

INDIAN OCEAN

Kimberley Plateau

3 Tanami Desert

Great Sandy Desert

A U S T

Lake Mackay

MacDonnell Ranges

Lake Amadeus

2

Uluru (Ayers Rock) ▲ **6**

Great Victoria Desert

Ashburton

Gascoyne

Lake Gairdn

Great Australian Bight

Cape Leeuwin **1**

INDIA

Skilled hoppers

6

There are 60 species of kangaroos living in deserts, cold regions, rain forests, and even on beaches! They have strong hind legs and long feet for hopping. They use their tail for balance. Males can grow to 6.5 feet (2 m) tall.

Kangaroos

7

Lethal jellies

Almost transparent, box sea jellies are the world's deadliest marine animal. Their 10-foot (3 m) long **tentacles** have stinging cells that become active when they make contact with prey or humans.

Box sea jelly

Deadly spider

The pea-sized female is responsible for most of the reported red-backed spider bites, some of which can be deadly. It is found all over Australia. Its web is funnel-shaped, with threads securing it to the ground. It can trap and kill prey larger than itself.

Koala

8

Leafy meals

A koala is a marsupial. Its diet and range are limited because it eats only some varieties of the 600 eucalyptus species. It rarely drinks water, getting most of its water from the leaves it eats.

9

Red-backed spider

New Guinea

Mount Wilhelm

Cape York

Great Barrier Reef

Cape York Peninsula

Great Dividing Range

Flanders

LIA

4

Great Artesian Basin

Warrego

8

Eyre rth

Lake Frome

ke rens

Darling

Lachlan

Murray

9

5 Mount Kosciuszko

Coral Sea

Forests of blue gum trees grow on the mountains of the Great Dividing Range.

EAN

Tasman Sea

Tasmania

Fact

Australia's ecosystem is so unusual because of its remote location. As a result, there are many animal species that occur here and nowhere else in the world.

Much of the North Island of New Zealand is used for grazing cattle and sheep.

NEW ZEALAND

North Island

Aoraki (Mount Cook) **10**

Southern Alps

South Island

10 ## Snow parrot

The kea is an inquisitive parrot that lives in New Zealand's South Island alpine regions. Its preferred food is beech leaves. However, in winter, it eats dead animals and has been recorded tearing at the flesh of weak livestock.

Kea

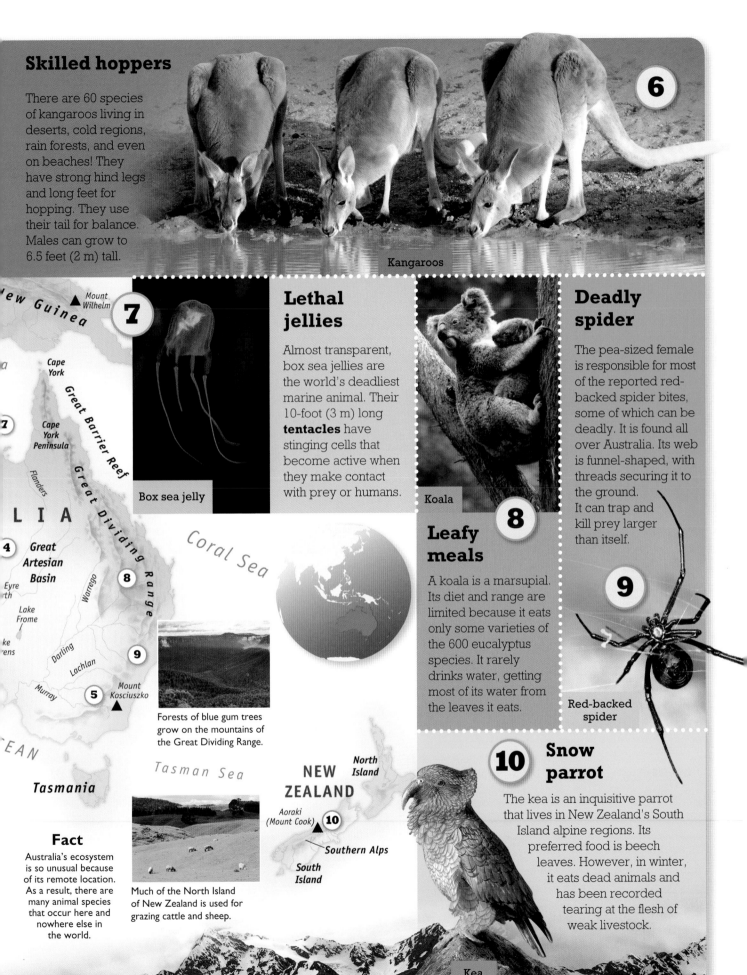

Great Barrier Reef

This is the largest living structure on the planet, stretching for almost 1,429 miles (2,300 km) along the coast of Queensland in the Coral Sea. It consists of more than 2,900 reefs and more than 1,000 islands and quays. Only a small amount of the reef is actually coral. The rest is inshore **mangroves**, sponge islands, sand **keys**, and deeper habitats. The reef is home to many species of fish, mollusks, sea snakes, sea stars, urchins, and whales.

Shady coral

1

This coral has a hard skeleton and is found in shaded waters on vertical surfaces, even shipwrecks. It fixes itself in place with a cement that it produces. At night, it extends its tentacles to catch plankton.

Orange cup coral

Reef eater

2

This sea star is one of a few animals that eat living coral. They feed by turning their stomach out through their mouth and digesting the coral's living tissue. They are covered in venomous spines that can cause great pain in humans.

Crown-of-thorns sea star

Fact

Some animals that live on the reef, such as turtles and crocodiles, have been around since prehistoric times. They have changed very little over time.

Cape York

Cape York Peninsula

The Great Barrier Reef is so huge it can be seen from space.

The giant clam is the world's largest mollusk.

A U S T R A L I A

Roaming turtle

3

This turtle gets its name from the color of its skin. Unlike most sea turtles, adults are **herbivores**, eating algae and sea grasses. The young turtles eat sea jellies, crabs, and sponges.

Green sea turtle

5

A clownfish and its anemone host

Shark of the reef

4

This reef shark has black tips on all of its fins. It lives in shallow warm water, and grows to almost 6 feet (2 m). It is not **aggressive** unless **provoked**. It has been seen to leap out of the water to go over shallow water in coral reefs.

Blacktip reef shark

Clowning around

This small, pretty clownfish coats itself in a slimy **mucus** that protects it from the anemone's poison. It hides among the anemone's tentacles to avoid predators and to feed on prey killed by the anemone.

Tasmania

Tasmania is the largest Australian island. Many animal species that have become **extinct**, or are on the verge of extinction, on the mainland survive in Tasmania. Almost half the land of this beautiful island is national parks and reserves. It contains the world's oldest trees and tallest flowering plants, along with many rare and unique animals, deep caves, and lakes. The most famous inhabitant of the island is the Tasmanian devil.

Tiny hunter

The little pygmy is the smallest of all possums at just 2–3 inches (5–6.5 cm). It is an agile climber but avoids the canopy to stay away from predator owls. This marsupial feeds on nectar, pollen, lizards, insects, and spiders.

1

Little pigmy possum

Noisy devil

2

Made extinct in the rest of Australia 400 years ago, this large, noisy **carnivorous** marsupial survives only in Tasmania. It leaves its den at night to hunt. The devil is named for its growls and screeches.

Tasmanian devil

Spiky coat

3

Covered in sharp spines, the echidna is an egg-laying mammal. When threatened, it rolls into a ball or digs a hole, leaving just its spines visible. Its claws tear at ant and termite nests looking for food.

Short-beaked echidna

Fact

Tasmania is also known as "Apple Isle." This is because, until recently, it was one of the main apple-growing areas in the world.

Bass Strait

Mount Olympus in Cradle Mountain–Lake St Clair National Park

King Island

Flinders Island

Cape Barren Island

Tasmanian wombat

Hiding in the bush

4

The red-bellied pademelon is only found in Tasmania. It seeks shelter in bushland, only coming to clearings at night to eat plants. This marsupial is related to wallabies and kangaroos. It has fur-covered ears, strong legs, and a fairly short tail.

5

Giant tunnels

This wombat—its closest relative is the koala—is an expert digger, creating tunnels 66 feet (20 m) long. It has short legs, large paws, long claws, and strong front teeth can chomp through any **obstructions**.

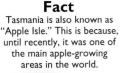
T A S M A N I A

Mersey

South Esk

2

3 *Lake Mackintosh*

Great Lake

Cradle Mountain

Lake St. Clair

1

Franklin

5

INDIAN OCEAN

Lake Gordon

Gordon

4

Lake Pedder

Huon

Tasman Sea

Red-bellied pademelon

Woodlands of Franklin-Gordon Wild Rivers National Park

Polar regions

The Arctic is mostly covered in frozen salt water. These ice packs drift on the currents of the deep Arctic Ocean. Large mammals, plants, and migrating birds thrive on tundra beyond the ice. The Antarctic—literally at the other end of the world —is the coldest place on the planet. It is mountainous and has active volcanoes. Because of its lack of rain, the ice-covered Antarctic is classified as a cold desert.

1 White predator

Nearly 10 feet (3 m) long, the polar bear has thick fur and a layer of blubber to keep it warm. It feeds on seals for their energy-rich fat. It makes epic swims in the search for food.

Polar bear

Arctic

Continents
Asia, Europe, and North America

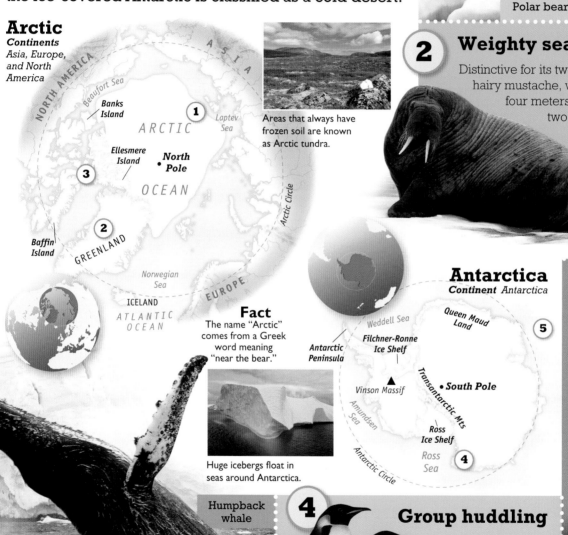

Areas that always have frozen soil are known as Arctic tundra.

Fact
The name "Arctic" comes from a Greek word meaning "near the bear."

Huge icebergs float in seas around Antarctica.

Antarctica
Continent Antarctica

2 Weighty seal

Distinctive for its two large tusks and hairy mustache, walruses grow to four meters long and can weigh two tons. They are very sociable, and will often snort and bellow at each other.

Walrus

Snowy fox 3

To prevent heat loss, the Arctic fox has fur even on its paws, a compact body, and short ears. It hunts lemmings, but also eats polar bear leftovers. Its superb hearing allows it to pinpoint the exact position of its prey.

Humpback whale

4 Group huddling

After a single egg is laid, female emperor penguins swim out to sea, only returning when the chicks hatch. Both parents take turns to provide the chick with food. Their diet consists mainly of fish, squid, and krill.

5 Enormous whale

Growing to 40–60 feet (12–18 m), this whale is stocky with long pectoral fins. It often comes out of the water (breaches) and slaps the surface with its fins or tail. Each year, it migrates from the Antarctic to waters off Central America.

Emperor penguins

Arctic fox

Learning More

Books

Burnie, David, *Animal: The Definitive Visual Guide to the World's Wildlife*, Dorling Kindersley, 2005

Howard, Jules, *The Animal World: The Amazing Connections and Diversity Found in the Animal Family Tree*, Blueprint Editions, 2018

Jackson, Tom, *The Illustrated Encyclopedia of Animals of the World*, Southwater, 2012

Jenkins, Steve, and Robin Page, *Look at Me! How to Attract Attention in the Animal World*, HMH Books for Young Readers, 2018

Kalman, Bobbie, *Where on Earth Do Animals Live?* Crabtree, 2018

Levine, Shar, *Animals: Mammals, Birds, Reptiles, Amphibians, Fish, and Other Animals*, Crabtree, 2010

Roper, Matt, *World's Weirdest Animals*, Summersdale, 2018

Websites

https://a-z-animals.com
A–Z Animals is an online animal encyclopedia containing information about a wide variety of animals from around the world.

https://kids.nationalgeographic.com/animals
This interactive website has information on reptiles, mammals, fish, insects, birds, and dinosaurs in various regions of the world.

www.sciencekids.co.nz/animals.html
Games, activities, and facts help you learn about animals and plants, food chains, bones and growth, plant and animal differences, and teeth and eating.

Glossary

adapted Changed to fit a new or specific use or situation
aggressive Ready or likely to attack or confront
agile Able to move quickly and easily
altitude sickness A sickness caused by lower oxygen levels at high altitudes
amphibian An animal that lives and breathes in water while young, then lives on land and breathes air as an adult
amplify To increase the volume of something
aquatic Of or relating to animals or plants that live in or near water
arid Very dry
blood vessel A tubelike structure that carries blood through the tissues and organs of the body
camouflage To hide or disguise the presence of something
canopy The uppermost trees or branches in a forest that form a nearly continuous layer of leaves
carnivorous Feeds on the bodies of other animals
coexist To live in relative peace together in the same place
cold-blooded Describing an animal that cannot control its body temperature and needs heat or sunshine to warm up
concave Curving inward, like a bowl
coniferous Describing evergreen trees that produce cones
crustaceans Animals that live in water and have hard shells and several pairs of legs
deciduous Describing trees that lose their leaves in the fall
deter To discourage a person or animal from doing something
diversity A wide variety of different things, peoples, or species
domestic Tamed and kept by humans as a work animal or pet

dung Animal droppings
efficient Achieving maximum productivity with minimal waste of effort or expense
elliptical Having an oval shape
elusive Difficult to find or catch
endangered Close to extinction or to dying out
evergreen Describing plants and trees that remain green year-round, even in winter
evolution theory Darwin's theory that organisms change over time as a result of changes in physical or behavioral traits that are passed on by their parents
extinct Describing a species, family, or other group of which there are no living members
fauna The animals of a particular region, habitat, or geological period
flora The plants of a particular region, habitat, or geological period
forages Searches over a wide area to find food
fungus An organism, such as mushrooms, that produces spores and feeds on organic matter
glacier A slowly moving mass or river of ice which is formed by the build up and compacting of snow, usually on mountains
habitats The natural home or environment of an animal, plant, or other living organism
hardy Capable of surviving through difficult conditions
herbivores Animals that eat plants
hibernation A condition of period of time in which an animal or plant spends the winter in a dormant (non-growing) state
keys Small low sandy islands on the surface of a coral reef
larvae The active immature form of an insect or other animal, which at birth or hatching looks very different from its parents

mangroves Dense areas of trees or shrubs that grow in tropical swamps, and have tangled roots above the ground
marsupial Describing animals that are carried and fed in their mother's pouch until fully developed
medicinal plants Plants that are used for medicinal purposes, to cure or lessen the symptoms of an illness
migration The seasonal movement of animals from one region to another
monsoon rains Heavy rains that are brought by strong winds between May and September in South and Southeast Asia
mucus A slimy substance produced by glands or tissues of the body
nocturnal Active at night
obstructions Things that block the way of something moving
offspring The babies or young of a living organism
outcrops A rock formation that is visible on the surface of the ground and is not covered by soil
peninsula A long piece of land that sticks out from a larger area of land into a sea or lake
plateaus Areas of raised land that is flat on top
plumage A bird's feathers
predators Animals that kill and eat other animals
provoked Made angry on purpose
pupa The inactive immature form of an insect between larva and adult; a chrysalis
reserve A place set aside for special use
rodents Animals that have two opposing sets of two front teeth for gnawing
roosts Settles onto a place, such as a branch, to sleep for the night
sanctuary A place of refuge or

safety; a nature reserve
savannahs Grassy plains with few trees, in tropical or subtropical regions
sensors Something that detects or measures a physical property, and records, indicates, or otherwise responds to it
shrubs A woody plant that is smaller than a tree
solitary Single; by oneself
steppes A larger area of flat treeless grassland in southeastern Europe or Siberia
temperate Characterized by mild temperatures
tentacles Slender flexible limbs or appendages on an animal that are used for grasping, moving around, or that contain sense organs
threatened Describing a species that is likely to become endangered in the near future
toxin A poison or venom from a plant or animal that will cause illness or death
tributaries Rivers or streams flowing into a larger river or lake
tropics The region between the Tropic of Cancer and the Tropic of Capricorn, where the weather is hot and humid
tundra The flat treeless Arctic region in which the ground is permanently frozen
unique One of a kind; unlike anything else
urinating Peeing
venom A poisonous substance secreted by animals such as snakes, spider, and scorpions through biting or stinging
wallowing Rolling around or relaxing in mud or water, usually to cool off or keep insects away
warm-blooded Describing animals that maintain a constant body temperature, no matter what temperature their surroundings are

Index